YALE HISTORICAL PUBLICATIONS